Y0-DBZ-537

Best New Chicano Literature 1986

Bilingual Press/Editorial Bilingüe

Address
Bilingual Press
Box M, Campus Post Office
SUNY-Binghamton
Binghamton, New York 13901
(607) 724-9495

Best New Chicano Literature 1986

Edited by
Julian Palley

Cenzontle:
Irvine Anthology No. 9
Ninth Chicano Literary Prize 1982-83

Bilingual Press/Editorial Bilingüe
BINGHAMTON, NEW YORK

ISBN: 0-916950-66-2

PRINTED IN THE UNITED STATES OF AMERICA

Cover design by Christopher J. Bidlack

Acknowledgments

This volume is supported by a grant from the National Endowment for the Arts, a federal agency.

The stories and poems in this collection represent the award winners from the Ninth Chicano Literary Contest sponsored by the Department of Spanish and Portuguese at the University of California, Irvine.

"The Scholarship Jacket," by Marta Salinas, which won honorable mention for short story, appears in *Nosotras: Latina Literature Today*, eds. María del Carmen Boza, Beverly Silva, and Carmen Valle (Binghamton, NY: Bilingual Press/Editorial Bilingüe, 1986).

Contents

Preface 7

Award Winners 8

JACK LOPEZ, The Boy Who Swam With Dolphins 9

LUIS J. RODRIGUEZ, Sometimes You Dance With a Watermelon 21

ELIZABETH NORIEGA STEIN, Chilpancingo, And the Need to Know 29

GUSTAVO CHAVANDO, Agustín, "El Bueno" 41

WILFREDO Q. CASTAÑO, Bone Games 51

Dedications, 51 / Poem From the Basement, 53 / Interluded Excerpt on Reality, 54

KATHLEEN J. TORRES, The Lantern of Her Caves 57

The Slaughtered Lamb Takes the Sealed Book, 57 / Street Faced Woman, 63 / May '79: Gas Line, 64 / Crazy, Your Heart or Mine? 64

LUIS MORONES CAREAGA, The Goddess Within Subterranean Women 65

Introduction, 65 / Dedication, 65 / Poems, 66-68

RICHARD ALEXANDER LOU, Works 69

Fanged Spit, 69 / One Morning With Resolve, Lissa, 71 / Untitleable, 72

GABRIEL DE ANDA, Poems 73

Jazz, 73 / I Captured an Angel, 78

Acknowledgments 83

Preface

This volume represents the publication of the award-winning stories and poems from the Ninth Chicano Literary Contest held at the University of California, Irvine. It is the product of the efforts of many persons—readers, coordinators, and friends of the contest—as well as, most importantly, the work of the many authors who submitted their writings. Over 200 manuscripts were received in the categories of short story and poetry. They were first evaluated by student and faculty readers within the University, and those considered best were then sent to a few outside judges, professors and Chicano writers, who made the final recommendations. Although to date the contest has been limited to citizens of the State of California, with succeeding editions it will be open to all citizens of the United States.

We are pleased that the Bilingual Review/Press has agreed to publish this and forthcoming volumes of the anthology, in this way allowing us a wider audience and the prestige accorded by the *imprimatur* of the Press.

For myself and for others involved in this process, in spite of the many frustrations that inevitably accompany the work of committees, this has been a most rewarding experience. It has resulted in the discovery of real talent in people of many occupations, of varying intellectual interests and social strata, and the creation of the means for their work to be presented to an interested public and their names to appear in print, often for the first time. All this carries with it its own satisfaction in the recognition that we are helping in the emergence of a long-obscured expression of a national, ethnic consciousness that is attaining a universal dimension.

Julian Palley, Editor

Award Winners

Short Story

First Place:	Jack López, "The Boy Who Swam With Dolphins"
Second Place:	Luis J. Rodríguez, "Sometimes You Dance With a Watermelon"
Third Place:	Elizabeth Noriega Stein, "Chilpancingo, And the Need to Know"
	Gustavo Chavando, "Agustín, 'El Bueno' "

Poetry

First Place:	Wilfredo Q. Castaño, "Bone Games"
Second Place:	Kathleen J. Torres, "The Lantern of Her Caves"
Third Place:	Luis Morones Careaga, "The Goddess Within Subterranean Women"

Honorable Mention

Short Story:	Marta Salinas, "The Scholarship Jacket"
Poetry:	Richard Alexander Lou, "Works"
	Gabriel de Anda, "Poems"

The Boy Who Swam With Dolphins

Jack López

Hussong's Cantina was a swarming mass of drunks overflowing out the front door and sometimes even out the large side windows that were open to let in the breeze off Ensenada Bay. Federales in their khaki uniforms would watch the action shaking their heads while sipping a cold beer that someone had given them. The cantina smelled of stale beer and dirt and piss and vomit and a little perfume from the few girls who were in there, and once in a while it would smell of tamales when a vendor would get brave and walk in carrying his steaming pot to try and weather the storm inside Hussong's. Then there would be yelling and whooping and the crowd would surge in a different direction and the vendor would scram out the door, protecting his goods from the crazies inside the bar. And through all this chaos Jesús gravitated to our corner and stood there smiling and then just staring at us.

As I look back after the passage of time, everything was so prophetic, so in order, so one two three, the way things sometimes appear after much thought; I can see that it was the excitement of our youth that set into motion a series of events that were never fully understood. And it is only now, after almost twenty years, that I must speak of what I saw.

Hussong's was surging back and forth like high tide in a very small bathtub and the old man picked us. Why us? But he did pick us and there is nothing to be done about that action for all of time. He managed to thread his way through the crowd and find us in the corner.

Jesús was the old man's name. He was very short, with a weather-beaten face like a man who has lived all his life in the sun and dark piercing eyes that seemed to burn an impression in your mind. He wore faded dirty Levis and torn leather sandals, and he had on a serape even in the heat of the afternoon.

"Buenas tardes," he said.

"Buenas tardes," good afternoon, I told him. He introduced himself and I introduced all of us to him. There was skinny Perry, who was the oldest and who had a brand new Volkswagen with a small oblong window in the back; there was tall, blue-eyed, blond-haired, rich Jay; Po, whose feet were so big that he could literally grab the edges of his surfboard to keep from falling off and who was so penniless that we all called him Po Boy; and myself, Juan, whose parents were camping on their vacation outside Ensenada. As I said, Perry was the oldest at seventeen while I was the youngest at fifteen. Maybe that was why we were off in the corner trying to be as inconspicuous as possible.

Jesús spoke a few words of English and between all four of us we spoke enough Spanish to drink beers with him the entire afternoon. You see, it was to be our last night in Baja California because school was going to start and my parents' vacation was coming to an end. So we drank with him and managed to find out that he was a fisherman. We told him that we were surfers in search of the perfect wave.

"I know, I see," he said.

"What do you mean?" Po Boy asked. "Have you seen a perfect wave?"

"Sí," he said, first pointing to his eyes and then to his head. "Sí."

But before we could get any further, a fight broke out. There was wild yelling followed by a surge of the crowd first into the bar and then away from the bar, coupled with the crash of breaking glass as some bodies flew out the windows just like in the old westerns. We couldn't see who was fighting, but when a shot was fired we were out the back door by the bathrooms and into the dirt lot that used to be next to Hussong's before the screaming stopped.

It was getting dark as paddy wagons pulled up to Calle Ruiz. The smell of food cooking was pushed along by a small breeze from the bay. We walked through the vacant lot and then crossed the street to López-Mateos. We walked down the street as the sound of shrieking whistles became more amd more faint. We went into a strip joint to get off the streets and the next recollection I have is of vomiting out the window of a speeding Volkswagen with September stars laughing at me as a thin overcast tried to sneak in off the ocean.

The following day we were all hung over. My father had heard us come back the night before. He was pissed.

"What are you guys, a bunch of animals?" he said. "You can help me break camp," he told me.

I don't think we could have surfed that day anyway. I helped my dad load the car while we all said our goodbyes. We would see them this evening. We only had a four hour drive to get back.

After my parents left we talked some and started to get our things together. The afternoon breeze was starting to pick up. The sand was hot from where we talked. We were in the center of a huge bay; Punta Banda was at the southern end, looking like Diamond Head in the glittering sun, and Ensenada was at the other end, with her harbor playing host to a few large tankers while three boats glided in under sail. The sand as far as you could see was a clean white with shimmering heat waves leading into a blue ocean. I picked up the shirt I had gotten sick in to wash it in the water. I felt something in the pocket. It was a small Hussong's coaster. I flipped it at Jay; it caught the wind and landed at his feet. Jay flung it at Po as I walked to the water. When I returned they were all gathered together holding the round coaster.

"It's a map," Perry said.

"A perfect wave," Po Boy said.

"What does that old Mexican know about waves," Jay said. "What does he know about anything?"

"Don't kid yourself, that old man knows a lot," Po Boy said.

"What are you guys talking about?" I asked.

"You didn't know?" Perry said.

"Know what?" I said.

"The old man," Jay said.

"What old man?" I asked.

"Jesús," Po Boy said. "He drew us a map on the back of that coaster."

"Let me see," I said. Sure enough, it was a crudely drawn map in pencil. "I never saw him draw anything, much less give it to me."

"We could surf a perfect wave," Po Boy said.

"It's not that far," Perry said.

"What are you talking about?" I asked. "School starts day after tomorrow."

"We could go there, surf that wave, and still be back in time for school," Po Boy fantasized.

"You're full of shit up to your ears," Jay said, as he started to eat a peanut butter and jelly tortilla.

"No, I'm not," Po said. "Look, this place is only eighty, maybe a hundred kilometers south at the most. We could be there in two or three hours."

"Yeah, but this map isn't drawn to scale," I said.

"It's not that far," Perry said. Jay was eating another peanut butter tortilla. I walked to the car. When I came back, some sort of agreement had already been reached.

"If everyone," they all looked at me, "wants to go, then I'll drive. But it has to be unanimous," Perry said.

"Look, I'd love to go but we told my parents," I said.

"By the time they get worried, we'll show up," Po Boy said.

"The way I figure it, we can surf this perfect wave all afternoon, sleep there, and be home tomorrow afternoon," Perry said.

"I'm game," Jay said, in between bites of his tortilla.

"There's nothing to be game about," I said, "We're not going."

"C'mon, Juan, don't be such a pussy," Po Boy said.

We tied the boards on the wooden racks and drove the dirt road to the highway. When Perry got to the highway he turned right, south, instead of heading north, the direction of home.

"C'mon, we'll just look at it," Perry said.

"All right, all right, let's go," I said. We were all equal partners in the conspiracy now. We drove past small adobe houses with white plumes of smoke rising from their chimneys. We drove through a valley of corn and then through another valley of olive trees swaying in the afternoon breeze.

We were approaching the checkpoint where travellers were supposed to have a visa to continue further south. Of course, none of us had visas. As we approached the wooden check house, we came upon an old hay truck fully loaded down. I mean, this was the straw that broke the camel's back. One more bale of hay and the truck would have collapsed. It looked like it was bowing in the center. Hay was flying off and dropping all over the highway as the truck struggled to keep moving. The checkpoint was getting closer and closer. Perry looked ahead and in his rearview mirror. As we were almost on the checkpoint, Perry went around the hay truck, slowed way down so that it blocked us from view, and then slowly pulled in front of the truck so that it still blocked us from view.

It could not have been done any better if it had been practiced. We waved thanks to the Mexicans in the hay truck and they waved back to us laughing. We were all jumping and yelling inside the cramped V.W. And thus began our trip in search of the perfect wave.

We had been driving for about an hour far away from the smell of the sea as the highway in Baja California headed inland. Hills and cactus and dry oven heat. Heat shimmering in waves far off down the road. Mirages of ocean waves. Then the highway began climbing up, up into the hills. After the road crested we came to an oasis by the side of the road. Perry coasted the car to a stop. This place was painted bright pink with huge green palms all around it. On the other side of the road there was a motel with a big green swimming pool. After we got close enough to the water we could see that the pool was green with algae. At the oasis there was a small veranda with a coke machine and chairs. We opened the top of the machine and took cold drinks. The owner came out from inside the building and smiled.

"You boys want some food?" he asked in good English.

"No thanks."

"How about some firecrackers?"

"No, we just want some drinks."

"You want to see a photograph?"

"A photograph? Sure." We thought it was naked girls.

"Twenty-five cents each," he said. He was a small, older man with grey hair, but he didn't seem that old, rather he was stately. His breath smelled of stale beer and he had not shaved for a few days so that grey whiskers reflected light when he turned a certain way. We followed him into the store. There was a fireplace in the center where a fat old lady was making tortillas by hand. The store was a curios shop and he had everything from stuffed iguanas to those cork guns that pop in your ear to playing cards with naked women on them. He even had switchblade knives in a display case. And all this was out in the middle of the desert. I guess he figured a bunch of real dumb tourists were going to come by.

Anyway, we followed him into a back room that had a brightly woven blanket for a door. It must have been his bedroom. There was a single metal framed bed in the center. Newspapers were spread over it and they were wrinkled as if someone had been lying on them. There was a small shrine in the corner with candles and a plaster of paris crucifix presiding over the room. He went to an old dresser that had a smokey cracked mirror over it, opened the top drawer, and took out an envelope. From the envelope came the photo. He showed it to us. It was a picture of a fat old man with a diaper on, lying on what looked like this same bed, in this same room.

"What the hell is going on?" Jay asked.

"Pancho Villa," said the old man. His eyes were glowing with pride.

"Pancho shit," Jay said and walked out. Perry followed, shaking his head.

"Pancho Villa on his death bed," the old man said. "Look closely." I tried to hold the photo but he wouldn't let go of it. Po Boy and I looked very close; there were all these marks all over this guy's belly, and it was a very big belly.

"Bullets," he said, his eyes big and gleaming, thinking of past times.

We bought a bunch of cold drinks and left the oasis. We drove on looking for three rocks on top of a hill and then shortly after that, a dirt road off to the right. About thirty minutes later we spotted the rocks. And sure enough, farther up the road there was a small dirt road leading into the arid hills but toward the ocean.

The road dropped into a valley that had water, a valley that had a series of farms. There were neat little pastures full of cows. We passed acre upon acre of olive trees swaying in the afternoon breeze. We passed dirt-floored houses where rounded ladies swept the dirt in their hand-embroidered dresses using brooms of straw. We drove on and on, crossing a shallow creek once, twice, then three times. It was getting late when finally the road emptied onto a broad floodplain that was bordered on both sides by steep hills covered with chaparral and cactus. We drove on. Then we could smell the salt, hear the sound of breaking waves. We drove over a dirt hill and we could feel the ground shaking from the power of the waves. Then the road took a turn to the right and we could see the waves. It was almost religious, like a miracle. Blue, blue sky with water a deeper blue. A small bay with a peak in the center. The entire bay was alight with diamonds sparkling from the afternoon sun. We thought at the time that the waves were at least fifteen feet, but now, after the passage of time, I know that they were no larger than ten feet. Still, that was the largest wave any of us had seen.

Jesús had been correct in his analysis of the wave that broke in this bay. It was perfect. It was a peak that broke both right and left in deep water but kept lining up all the way into a very fast shorebreak.

Po Boy was in the water paddling out before any of us had our boards off the car. We were hesitant, not knowing what the bottom was like or what else was going to be in the water with us. But soon we were all in the water doing what we did best—surfing. We were taking off on the largest waves we had ever seen and riding them like we did it every day. The bottom was large, smooth river stones that did not hurt your feet. It was funny, but as you rode into the shorebreak, the water rushing back out from the beach would clank the stones together, making it sound as if there were an audience clapping. All of us rode some pretty fantastic waves, but we all got blasted at one time or another. Like the set that came just before sunset which closed out the entire bay. It kept building on the uneven horizon. I was so scared my heart almost popped out my mouth. Perry had lost his board trying to roll under one of the first waves to break. Jay was way inside when the set hit. So it was just Po Boy and myself. I was farther out than he was, but he was not scared, rather he had never seemed to be having such a great time. The huge waves made him come alive. I looked down the face of one smoking giant that I just barely made it over and saw Po Boy bail off his board and body surf the drop, shouting at the top of his lungs.

The explosion after the wave broke was tremendous, somewhat like a waterfall. I didn't think I would see Po Boy alive again, but there he was in almost the same position on the next wave yelling his head off. He amazed me, it was a Po Boy that I had never before seen . . .

It had been pretty late when we arrived, so we only got to surf about two hours before darkness overtook our magical bay with the perfect wave. We were exhausted after the short time of surfing with so much adrenalin flowing. We built a fire of driftwood on the beach and warmed up some tortillas and beans and drank some warm cokes. We fell asleep under a sky that was not competing with electricity to show us its charms. We were definitely smug in the knowledge that we had searched out and found what for us was a perfect wave.

The next morning I awoke to find my sleeping bag completely wet. The fog was in. And it was a thick fog. A slight movement was blowing in from the ocean, pushing small droplets of water past my face. Perry and Jay were still asleep. Po Boy was not in his sleeping bag. I arose, stretched, put on my Levis and sweatshirt, and walked over to the bushes. I came back and cut some kindling to start a fire. The newspaper was damp but finally I got some small flames going. I fed the flames some larger pieces of driftwood and soon had a fire. I boiled water for coffee. Jay and Perry awoke separately, used the facilities, shall we say, and then took coffee with me.

"Where's Po Boy?" asked Jay.

"His board's gone, so I guess he's out there surfing," I said.

"He's nuts."

"I don't know if it's balls or lack of brains."

We warmed some tortillas on the fire. Jay spread peanut butter and jelly on his and then rolled them like they were big cigarettes. Perry and I put butter on ours. We drank our coffee in the stillness of early morning fog. All we could hear was the roar of crashing waves. It was strange that the water was so close yet you could not see it, but only hear waves breaking. After a while Perry walked to the water and started yelling for Po Boy.

As it became later we could see that the fog was hugging the coast. Inland it was bright and clear, on its way to becoming hot once again. Yet the fog still clung to the ocean so that we could not see the waves or Po Boy. We all wanted to go. We loaded the car. Perry started the engine thinking that Po could hear it and he would come in. Perry honked the horn over and over. We walked to the water's edge and shouted again and again. Evidently he could not hear us. It wasn't like Po to completely disregard us. We walked up and down the beach looking for his surfboard. No sign. We were all thinking the same thing but no one would bring it up. If only the fog would lift. But it wouldn't.

It was afternoon when we finally left. We drove back to Ensenada. We arrived in town and went straight to the Bahia Hotel. I placed a long-distance call to my parents. It took about a half hour for the call to go through. I told my father what had happened. He was stunned.

"I don't think he drowned, Dad, he's too good a swimmer," I said.

The line was full of static so I had to speak loud, almost yelling. "I think he just got disoriented by the fog. He just went the wrong way on the beach and couldn't find us. It was just the fog, Dad. We're going back to look some more." He told us to come home, that we had done all that we could for now. He said he would call the American Consulate. The manager of the hotel told us not to worry. He told us that the Federales would find him if he were alive.

We drove home in the golden dusk of September, end of summer Baja. I had a lump in my throat most of the way home and I guess Jay and Perry did too, because not much was said.

The next day was school. My second year of high school. Rooms that smell only of new Levis. Scrawny girls all made up. Everyone at school wanted to hear the story. I left after my second period class during snack break. I walked down to the beach and watched the waves break. I didn't even feel like surfing. Farther down the road I saw Perry sitting in his car all alone, watching the ocean.

Two days passed and still there was no word of Po Boy one way or the other. It took me that long to talk my dad into going back. And then it was only because I told him I was leaving in the morning even if I had to take the bus.

We left about four in the morning. We ate breakfast in San Diego. We stopped in Ensenada and had some coffee and pan dulce. It was about ten-thirty when we arrived at the oasis. We sipped on cold cokes and looked at Pancho Villa again.

The station wagon made it nicely through the creek. My father was not too happy about driving his car on a surf trip, but under the circumstances he could not have said anything even had he wanted to. We passed the same cows, the same brightly dressed ladies sweeping out their dirt houses. Finally we drove up and over that small dirt hill, revealing the most captivating waves I have ever seen.

The fog was gone, the surf was down, but the smaller waves were still perfect. I started wishing that I had brought my board and then remembered why we had returned. I took my shirt off and began running toward the south point, looking back, watching my father get smaller and smaller. At the end of the point I climbed the dirt hill and walked over the top. I walked through the chaparral and cactus to the other side of the point. Below there was another bay, somewhat larger, with waves breaking in it. There was a surfboard on the beach. I yelled to my father and then went down to the beach to see where Po Boy was. I thought that there would be footprints leading to a small shack where Po Boy would be resting in a hammock. It was not so. My father finally made it to the beach.

"I thought the Federales were going to search the beaches?" I asked my dad. He made no answer.

"Well, at least I was right about the fog turning him around. He went to the wrong beach." Still my father said nothing. He knew enough about the ocean to know that a riptide could have taken Po's board around to that cove.

We searched the cove and then went one more before we started working our way north. We came upon a small village that was built right on the beach and which was surrounded by light little wooden dories that were all tied together with an old thick rope. The few dogs that were around the village greeted us with growling and barking, but later I could pet some of them. The villagers were small dark people who were very reserved and polite. My father speaks Spanish, so he told the men our story as we squatted in a circle in the shade of a palapa. The men looked gravely at each other. They told my father they had seen nothing out of the ordinary. They offered us food and we had a dinner of tortillas, beans, and a really good fish stew.

We walked a few coves back to where we had left the car. The sun was going down through a few sparse clouds shooting golden rays directly at us. I asked my father if I could go surfing before it got dark and he said absolutely not. It made me feel a bit like the girl who runs away with her boyfriend and then gets caught. After that her parents keep her locked inside her room so that nothing bad will happen to her reputation.

Through begging and pleading I got my father to spend the night there. We had sleeping bags and we folded the seat down in the station wagon and slept in the car. I couldn't sleep much because I felt that Po Boy was close by. I left the car just after five in the morning. It was not yet light but was no longer night. I started working my way north, back toward the village. I made it two coves up; the sun was threatening to come out from behind the mountains in the east, and I could feel the heat. I was on top of a point looking down onto the next cove. An army truck pulled up in a cloud of dust at the other end of the cove. Two soldiers jumped out from the back of the truck with their machine guns raised. Twelve men slowly climbed off the truck. The driver of the truck and another soldier emerged from inside the cab. It appeared that the twelve men were prisoners because they were bound at their hands and feet with rags. One soldier slung his machine gun over his shoulder and began untying the prisoners. His partner kept his gun on the men. The two soldiers from the cab were talking and laughing and drinking something, maybe coffee. After the twelve men were untied they began taking off their clothes. When they were completely naked they were forced to face the ocean with their hands above their heads. The guards raised their machine guns. The sun was coming over the mountains making the beach light up as if there were a film being shot. All of a sudden the soldiers began firing their guns in the air. I yelled but they couldn't hear because of all the noise. The prisoners ran in twelve different directions, all away from the soldiers. The two men watching roared with laughter, rocking back and forth on their heels, holding their bellies.

I turned and ran from there. I ran all the way to the cove where we had found the perfect wave. On the south point I saw Jesús in the same clothes, the same serape, that he had had on in Hussong's. I called to him. He pointed to the ocean. I looked down to the water and saw a school of dolphins playing in the waves. As they swam on the face of the breaking wave I could hear them chattering. I called to Jesús again. He motioned to the waves with his head. Another wave was rising higher than any of the other ones. There was a dolphin riding along with something else. It was too light to be a seal. It caught up to the dolphin, went underneath it, and then broke the surface right by the tube, just ahead of the white water, went to the top of the wave and dropped back down over and over again always ahead of the white water. I called to Jesús but he was no longer there. I ran back to the car. My father was still sleeping. I took Po Boy's board from underneath the car, put on my trunks, and paddled out. Dolphins were taking off and riding crisp blue waves all around me. One nudged my board almost knocking me off, all the while chattering like he was trying to tell me something.

A set of waves appeared on the horizon. I paddled farther out, turned Po's board around and took off on the first wave of the set. I took the drop and bottom turned, came up to the top, stalled, walked forward, trimmed, and rode into the shorebreak. The shorebreak walled up and I moved closer to the nose, crouched, and stretched my left foot almost over the nose of the board. It felt like I was airborne in green air. I was flying, I was weightless. The wave started to throw out over me, to wrap me within itself, and just at that last instant before oblivion, a form came speeding out from deep inside the tube to catch me as if I were not even moving. At first I thought it was a dolphin but it was transparent and there was no dorsal fin. We were frozen together face to face for that instant and I knew that it was Po Boy. But he had gone through a metamorphosis; his eyes had a film over them, his arms seemed to be connected to his body, and even his huge feet were connected as he flashed by me. In that one eternal instant, I know he smiled at me before he shot off like a shooting star. Before the wave slammed me to the bottom I saw Po undulating far off in the tube, free from the bounds of ordinary speed.

Spent, I swam in. My father was on the beach holding Po Boy's board.

"Dad, he's not dead!" I screamed, "He's swimming with the dolphins."

My father would not let me go back in the water. After a short time of trying to show my father which dolphin was Po, Jesús came paddling through the bay with slow, steady, powerful strokes in his beat-up dory. He paddled out beyond the south point, and as if he were a shepherd and the dolphins were his flock, they all left the bay. The waves even seemed to quiet down. Tears were streaming down my face but I wasn't sad, rather I was so happy for Po.

We returned home and I would not change my story. The doctor said I was suffering from complete exhaustion and maybe a nervous breakdown. I felt fine, I wasn't sad. They made me stay in bed for two weeks but I would still not change my story. They even went so far as to bring in a marine biologist who told me that sometimes a school of dolphins will swim with a drowned body. I listened to him and then calmly told him he was full of shit and to get out of my room.

And now, after almost twenty years have passed, I still feel exactly the same way that I felt that early morning so long ago. Sometimes when I watch sunsets at the beach I think of my friend and of all the waves he has surfed in his endless migrations.

After all, wolves have raised human babies, haven't they?

Sometimes You Dance With a Watermelon

Luis J. Rodríguez

The early morning sunlight sneaked into the dark cluttered bedroom through a number of small holes in the aluminum foil that covered every window. Susana had placed the foil there so her husband, Pete, could sleep during the bright warmness of day.

She slowly began to turn away from the heavy and sleep-laden figure on the bed, as Pete lay curled up in a fetal position.

Pete worked the graveyard shift at a foundry near their home in the Florencia barrio of the south side. He slept during the day and worked nights until he managed his way home from the heat and chatter of the blast furnaces to the comfort of his house and Susana's warm body.

Susana got out of the covers and slowly put on her dirty pink bathrobe. She tiptoed toward the door and opened it to a frustrating tune of creaky hinges, ever mindful of Pete's restless sleep as he turned into another position but did not awaken.

She knew too that there was little to wake a body as torn down as Pete's from a scorching and brutal night at the foundry.

She walked into the living room, where on several mattresses lay her children, her sister Sybil, and her sister's no-good, always-out-of-work husband Stony.

She managed to step over the bodies on the floor on her way to the kitchen. This life was draining life from her. But it was all she could hang on to since she first came from Oaxaca, Mexico, just after her daughter Chela was born some 10 years ago, when she was but 16 years old.

Sneaking across the California border was not as difficult, it seemed, as having to stay in Los Angeles' dingiest apartments with a small child, no husband, and no livable skills. And dumped into a strange world of sounds and bright lights and people who never say anything to you unless you act crazy like those on downtown streets.

Susana went into the kitchen to prepare something to eat. Those days in Florencia were filled with non-fat powdered milk for breakfast, tortillas and butter for lunch, and corn flakes for dinner.

She opened a cupboard as cucarachas scurried away to darker places. The bare shelves could not answer the calls from her stomach or those of her children, although she honestly did not feel the same concern for Sybil or Stony. She felt certain they were into drugs and illegal movidas of some sort.

Why her darling sister would end up with an ex-con like Stony was beyond her. Sybil, in many ways, was the more restrained of the two when they were younger, although a strain of craziness between them was very evident. But ever since Susana helped her across the border and into the city, Sybil began to hang out at the nightclubs off Spanish Broadway and meet some unstable characters. One of whom gave her the two children she bore. But the worst being the one she brought home one day and eventually married, Stony.

Stony actually seemed nice. But when he talked, his missing front teeth and his constantly shifting eyes gave off an ominous look, something that Susana noticed in a lot of Chicanos just out of the joint. Let alone that he never worked but, when pushed, would somehow come up with bread and beer money.

"Chingao, nunca hay nada de comer," Susana muttered, as the empty cupboards began to focus in her eyes. She didn't mind the adults not eating, but the children had to eat. She was prepared to starve if the children could eat.

The frustration was weighed down by the fact that Pete worked long and hard to maintain the small, one-bedroom place for Chela and Pete's two smaller children from a previous relationship, as well as Sybil, Stony, and her sister's two children. But with the rent, utilities, and essentials, including emergencies that always seemed to happen, there was just not enough for everything all the time.

In the winter, all five children would gather up close on one of two mattresses, letting the warmth of their small bodies bring them to sleep, while Sybil and Stony shared the other one.

On summer nights, they slept with the covers off and windows opened—their only air conditioner.

Her hunger unsatisfied, Susana closed the cupboard and walked toward the kitchen window that overlooked an alley behind their home on Miramonte Street.

From behind a torn screen, old paint peeling from the wood frame, Susana peered at several children playing in the alley.

Her hair was disheveled and long as she leaned against the window. She looked over the haze of the Los Angeles sky. The children in their play yelled in broken English, half-Spanish, and a language of their own.

One small child was quiet, playing by himself with beaten up trucks and limbless army men, oblivious to the rest of the world.

"Está loco," Susana thought.

And she thought what a strange place this Florencia was. So much noise; factory whistles heard at intervals along with the continuous pounding of machinery. There was a lot of tension in the streets, with souls that were taunt and ready to snap. Two drunken men walked by just then as she gazed. They sat on the edge of a curb to partake in a short dog.

Family quarrels became battlegrounds, with children running and screaming out of households and police cars turning sharply around corners.

Although life in Susana's Oaxacan village was poor and in want, it was not so complicated. But she thought of that and at the same time accepted that she would never go back. This was her life now, she thought. With Pete, with the children, and even with her sister and Stony. In barrio Florencia. Looking at days on end, as men in the garment plants brought scraps of clothes for her neighbors to sew, often into the wee hours of the morning. No, she could never go back.

But she began to think, "If I have to die, let me die in Mexico. Bury me deep in Oaxaca. In my red hills, in the cactus fields and rain forest of el Istmo de Tehuantepec. Bury me in my long hair, in braids. Bury me in my long Zapoteca skirts. Bury me among the ancients, among the brave, strong, and tall ones. On my land. Remembering I had traveled new grounds. Opened up new worlds. That I had lived in North America."

She thought of Pete, sleeping and working his life away. A good man. So hard to find, Sybil always said. Yet, Pete was truly decent. Working nights and double shifts. Tapping a beat with a large vertical jackhammer and then clearing tuyeres with long metal bars. But he was always tired.

Susana needed to get away this morning. The morning called her, beckoning her to get out and do something. Go someplace, anyplace.

She could borrow Stony's beat-up Ford pickup and visit the old furniture stores and used clothes stores along Vermont Avenue or go all over the south side gathering newspapers, cartons, junked car parts or whatever to sell at the county dumpsite in South Gate.

She had done it so many times that the men at the dump got to know her quite well. They looked forward to her happy and brash approach, the way she explained things in her broken and Spanish-ridden English. Listening to her many schemes.

Susana got dressed quickly. She gathered a few items of money and junk and stuffed it into an old leather purse. She walked over the bodies stretched out on the mattresses to where Chela was sound asleep. She looked at the closed eyelids and fingered the child's small hand.

Susana gently shook the girl from her sleep.

"Amá," Chela moaned. "¿Qué pasó?"

"Come with me, Chela," Susana said. "I need you to help me."

Chela could barely make out her mother's face. She thought, oh no, she wants me to steal old beaten furniture from the back of Goodwill trucks again.

"Oh, Amá. I'm tired," she complained.

"Mira no más. You're tired, eh. You ain't done nothing. You don't clean or anything. Now get dressed and come with me," and with that Susana stormed into the kitchen.

Chela grumbled and cursed, but she threw her blankets off, unmindful of the other children next to her, and rolled off the mattress.

Mamá is stubborn, she thought. There is no moving her at all.

Chela swaggered into the bathroom while her mother prepared a couple of tacos to be eaten later.

"What are we going to do, Amá?" Chela inquired as she attempted to brush her hair into some kind of shape. She had grown feisty at her age and, unlike her mother, refused to wear braids. Just long hair, wavy and free-flowing on her head.

"Adiós, adonde quiera Dios. What's it to you," Susana yelled.

"Gee, I was just asking," Chela said. It would go back and forth like that frequently between her and her mother.

Susana hurried outside to check the truck. The empty cupboard was a contrast to the driveway that overflowed with old bike parts, boxes of yellowed newspapers, and rain-soaked cartons. She managed to reach the truck and get inside. It grinded and griped but eventually it turned over with smoke filling the cluttered driveway.

"Vámonos, muñeca," she yelled for Chela over the truck's engine. "¡A la volada!"

By then other members of the family were awake. Stony was the first to pop his head through a window and curse Susana about gunning the engine so hard. But Susana just pressed the accelerator more as the smoke thickened behind the truck.

No sleepy-eyed, ex-pinto, and drunk of a brother-in-law was going to ruin her beautiful summer day, she thought. A day that begged for her to do something. Anything.

Chela flew out of the house, banging the torn-up screen door behind her. Susana backed the truck out and Chela yelled as she desperately jumped into the passenger side while it clamored out the driveway and onto Miramonte Street.

They continued down the street with smoke trailing from behind and Stony cursing from the window.

"¡La loca mendiga!" he yelled.

The rickety Ford roared onto Florence Avenue and toward Alameda Street as old Mexicans sold fruit at the roadside from even worse beaten trucks while factory workers gathered in front of chain link fences for the "garbage" wagons of food to arrive for their morning break.

Susana decided to go to el centro—downtown Los Angeles, the hemispheric dumping ground of the Latin people. No English spoken here.

Once into downtown's skid row, warehouses, and garment plants, Susana pulled into the heavy traffic of cars and people on Spanish Broadway as old black preachers yelled sermons from the sidewalks with bibles in their hands.

Bootblacks and newspaper vendors on a number of corners studied the many characters they catered, scanners of the latest news from

Mexican publications and the cut-up bodies and closeup shots of dead people in the "Alarma" crime and murder magazines.

"How about a shine . . . shoe shine . . . para zapatos," yelled a half-blind young man.

The streets bristled with the hardened souls as well as the families and the single mothers shopping. They came from countless havens of misery. Each soul with a story.

Hundreds gathered in front of a Spanish theatre bearing the names of Mexican actors and actresses. Norteña and salsa music poured out of stores.

A drunk pulled out from a Tejano norteña bar, followed by another man. The second man knocked the first one to the ground and repeatedly punched him in the face. Nobody stopped or did anything.

Another man pulled a little boy from the crowd and had him pee into the gutter.

Susana and Chela cruised further up Broadway and its crowded intersections; cholos stood by alleyways, old ladies walked slowly with heavy bags, winos lay in their vomit, gray-haired derelicts pushed shopping carts full of trash . . . the rapid-fire Spanish voices, noisy trucks unloading merchandise, and the foul-smelling, smog-ridden buses loading people.

Susana noticed an empty parking spot and manuevered into it. On the side was a sign that read, "TOW ZONE." But she left the truck there anyway.

"Amá, the sign says . . ." Chela started to say. But she soon saw it was not going to do any good. Susana had already walked away, as if by ignoring it the sign would not exist.

"Damn her," Chela muttered and ran up behind her.

The day was hot, the walks were long, and the browsing and arguing over items, most of which Susana had no intention of buying, began to take its toll. Susana made shopping around too much like work, Chela concluded.

"It's so hot. How about a watermelon, mija," Susana said.

"Sure, I go for that," Chela beamed.

They stopped at a fruit stand. In front of them were laid out papayas, mangos, apples, and oranges from Mexican and Californian fields.

They picked out a dark, green, large watermelon. Susana argued with a man on the price, but she finally gathered her change and paid for it.

Chela attempted to carry the watermelon that she estimated was a quarter her size.

The weight of the watermelon, the cluster of people, the heat and noise; all of it became unbearable.

They stopped to rest a little by a bus stop bench.

Chela looked at her mother and said, "I'm tired, Amá. The sandía is too heavy."

Susana stood up. Then she thought about Oaxaca and about a time when she was a little girl. She thought about how Sybil and she would carry bundles and baskets of clothes and food on their heads. Then her thoughts vanished and her eyes turned to the watermelon weighing down her daughter.

Susana took the watermelon from Chela, who in turn gave out a deep sigh of relief.

Susana walked a little further, then stopped. With care, she tried to place the watermelon on her head. Slowly, she removed her hand. It wobbled a little, almost falling. She grabbed it again, then let go slowly while attempting to balance it. She then began a few steps. It did not fall, still on top of her head.

Chela looked at her mother horrified.

Then Susana began to dance.

A crowd gathered around as she danced past the Broadway stores, immigration offices, and clothing and record stands. Merchants stepped out of their businesses, preachers stopped their incantations, and people at bus stops strained their necks to look. Horns beeped, hands waved and others simply got out of the way.

Susana had remembered how to balance the load as she had done years ago as a little girl.

She began to rumba to a cumbia beat coming from a record store. She laughed and others laughed with her. Chela stepped aside and stared in amazement as well as embarrassment. Está loca, she thought, and shook her head.

"Ahhhjjjiii," her mother yelled out.

She had not looked so happy in a long time, amid the bustling noise of the central city, among her people, shadowed by the tall Victorian buildings.

Susana weaved into stores and throngs of shoppers with the

watermelon still on her head. Remembering a time when life was simple and direct on a rancho in Oaxaca.

Chilpancingo, And the Need to Know

Elizabeth Noriega Stein

My aunt Nora stands waiting. She's not waiting for us at the plane, as expected, but just beyond Customs. In her arms she carries a dozen red roses, their edges brown and beginning to curl at the tips: Mexico, or at least how I've come to think of it—part delight, part dismay. Nora leans toward me and presses the flowers nearer. Her powdered cheek brushes mine and her lips mime a kiss; it wouldn't do to mark me with her lipstick.

The conversation begins in Spanish, and I feel quickly forgotten. Sensitive to any exchange between my mother and her sister Nora, I notice their stiff embrace, my mother's hurt look, and the quick movement of her hands as she fusses with her hair, jacket, and collar. I want to grab those busy hands and tell her not to be afraid, not to be angry—even though fear and anger are things to which she would never admit. I watch silently, wondering if this conciliatory trip to Mexico is such a good idea after all. Pilar and Nora, estranged sisters united once again upon the death of my Anglo father. It has a nice ring. Maybe now Mother will allow herself to be Mexican.

"Kiss your aunt," Mother commands me in English.

"I did!" "She did!"

Nora and I respond simultaneously, and I seem to catch the same annoyed yet imploring tone in our voices. Nora is over 50 years older than me, and I guess it's the weight of those years that gives her both the authority and the urgency to make the peace. Mother seems less willing, full of bridling reserve. I piece together what I can with my broken understanding; I wish I knew why it had to be like this.

Once again they begin to speak Spanish. Mother smiles and chatters as we walk to the car, but it's her public, aggressive self I see, and I'm disgusted. She doesn't want them to think she's a poor-little-old-widow-come-begging, and so instead she's defiant. We fall into single file: my aunt leads the way, then my mother; I trail behind them, and a porter follows me. Already there is something funereal about our meeting—the acknowledgement of grief, perhaps, added to the fading roses and this processional walk. We are all so unhappy with each other.

"Come to Mexico," my aunt told me when I was little. "See what it's really like. Your mother only tells you the bad things."

I'll come, my time of arrival the awakening from my newest dream: an attic door opening to reveal a stockpile of Mesoamerican sculpture—squat figurines with hands on knees and forward-smiling faces, covered with dust yet neatly arranged, row upon row, shelf upon shelf, towering ever upwards into the dim attic recesses. Nearer, within arm's reach, is a smooth wooden cabinet. Carved onto its only knob is a woman's face: it is her delight to open the door.

But then I wake up, because this is, after all, only an anthropological, book-bound dream.

My cousin Fabián and his four sons meet us at the car. Fabián kisses me in an offhand manner and helps to haul our bags into the trunk of the fishtailed black Cadillac. My mother cues me—sit in the back—and I climb in between Nora and Fabián's son, Sandro. I resent her pointed finger but pretend to humor her, wasting an arch look on Sandro, who is an uncomprehending eight years old. (They're raising him wrong, Mother has said. They idolize him because he's blond with green eyes; he'll turn out to be a snob, you wait.) Sandro regards my tan face for one grave moment and then smiles.

"Kees," he says, puckering.

"He has a crush on you," my aunt informs me.

His sly attention pleases me and I plant a fat, Straight-Ahead-Red kiss on him. His brothers squeal with pleasure when they see the tattoo; now they all want it. My mother glances back with an oddly triumphant look. She drops her hand over the seat and wiggles her fingers—this means I am to take her hand, which I do. Nora seizes my other hand and I am a sudden link between the Spanish in front and the carefully phrased, interrogative English in back. I've come to Mexico to speak English with my Mexican aunt, and my mother's come to show off her Americanismo in Spanish. Together we look like three peas in a Mendelian pod: my mother dark, my aunt fair, myself somewhere in between.

"And you are happy to be here?" Nora asks me declaratively, stroking my hand. Next to my lively, suspicious mother, Nora looks slow and faded, with ash-colored hair and eyes. She moves with melancholic deliberation, like a connoisseur weary of making distinctions. She asks me about my studies and reminds me that all her children were educated in the United States. Nora, in fact, has spent much of her life there; she will see to it that her grandchildren go there too. This whole business about the need to look and act American—which means to be fair-skinned and speak English—was this a product of Mexico, or was it something my mother and her family acquired in the States?

Then I remember Isabel, my namesake. Unlike Nora, she is not a step-sister, but closer to my mother in age and coloring. Had she lived she would've been 64 today, instead of the seventeen-year-old she will always remain. I try to imagine what she would've been like, aging her through adulthood on the basis of one photograph. Isabel died in a car accident one similar summer, winding through the mountains on the way to Acapulco. Nora's boyfriend was driving while Isabel and Nora took turns singing to keep him awake. Mother, 15, lay asleep in the back seat with the suitcases. (Later the suitcases would be what she would remember most—the tumbling suitcases.) But what of Isabel, carried down in an Indian blanket to a foothill town with an unpronounceable name, Chilpancingo? (Everyone loved Isabel, my mother told me. Everyone in Mexico; everyone in the States. Pilar loved her; Nora loved her. She was so beautiful and so good.) Isabel, I suspect, had been dark—but not dark enough to be offensive. Isabel, the acceptable bridgeway between Pilar and her half-sister Nora, lay dying before them in Chilpancingo. I think of that scene and I roll the Indian name around in my mouth like an oily marble; I want to see them in Chilpancingo, beyond Isabel's death: two half-sisters, regarding each other with—? Today there is a new meeting ground for Nora and my mother, Pilar.

You're Pilar's, one will say, but I can love you.

She's dark, the other will answer, but she's lovely.

What right had my mother to make me her apology, her defense? And who was my aunt to deign to accept me, but not my mother?

* * *

We arrive at my aunt's colonial, six-bedroom house, and there are many people waiting to meet us. All of the introductions are in Spanish. I wish they weren't; I'm tired, and it's even harder to understand. Between nods and handshakes I glance around the entrance hall. An ornate stairway curls upwards, its gilded handrail chipping away in spots, showing black paint underneath. The stairs are carpeted in dark blue velvet, a worn white trail snaking up the center. My aunt Nora pulls me through the crowd into an enormous living room. Everything is a somber dark blue: blue walls, blue drapes, blue velvet rug, even a blue velvet sofa. I edge toward the sofa, but Nora pulls me determinedly through the room and down two steps into a wood-paneled rehearsal room. We are on tour.

"Here are the trophies," she smiles.

Gold records line the walls of this square, furnitureless room, and my uncle Ricardo's publicity photos are everywhere. If Nora is pale and deliberate, Ricardo is larger-than-life, barely aging from photograph to photograph: Ricardo with Bob Hope; Ricardo at the race track; Ricardo at MGM; Ricardo at the Copacabana. In every photograph Ricardo has his guitar. "I'll play you a song," he told me once. "You tell me if it estinks."

"Señora," a thin voice calls. My aunt and I turn to face a small, nut-brown woman with sharp bones and a pointed chin. She wears a faded print dress, her black hair pulled back into a long braid. She is la criada, the maid. She speaks submissively to my aunt, casting shy glances my way. My smiling curiosity is too much; reluctantly my aunt makes introductions.

I know about the criadas of Mexico, how they sleep in closet-sized rooms and work for almost nothing. More than an occupation, la criada is an insult to be hurled at the dark, the poor. It is best said dismissively: "Hija de la criada." Daughter of the maid. We know where you come from.

We strike a tableau: la criada and I, shaking hands, my aunt watching. The maid smiles but shrinks from my handshake, retreating with her eyes on my aunt. I have managed to embarrass the three of us at once.

"Nora!"

My mother breaks the scene. She looks angry. "We're tired," she says, "We need to freshen up from the trip."

"Of course!" My aunt agrees, unperturbed. "Right after I show my niece the house. Then I'll do whatever you like—drive you to your hotel, whatever . . . Whatever you like, dear."

That cool "dear" grates on my mother, yet here she can do little under Nora's subtle hand. Even the offer to drive us to a hotel has implications, because in families of real affection separate lodgings would never be discussed. Nevertheless, my aunt takes my arm and we glide past, up the stairway.

"Where's Ricardo?" my mother calls after us. "Will we see him?"

My aunt stops but does not turn around.

"I sent my husband on an errand. I don't know when he'll be back."

Four beats, maybe five, with nothing to do or say to break the intangible warfare between Pilar and Nora. We move on, and I let my eyes climb from frame to frame, publicity stills lining the stairway, image and pretense.

* * *

Upstairs, Nora leads me with the formality of an official guide. The house is very large—from the upper windows I can even see a tennis court in the backyard—yet everything seems in a state of disrepair. Nora pulls me into the semi-darkness of what appears to be a closet, situated tunnel-like between two bedrooms. There are many shelves on either side, with many articles neatly arranged, row upon row, shelf upon shelf. One of the shelves holds an assortment of faded photographs and holy cards. Rosaries are draped over framed portraits; black-wicked candles are clustered before them. The house chapel; the prayer closet! Here, as elsewhere in the house, there is the feeling of decay: the rosary beads are chipping, the glass-covered photos are gathering dust. My eyes run over the pictures, most of them unfamiliar. Except one . . .

The scene is American, etched out in the gaudy Kodak-color of 1950: it is my parents' wedding reception at Clifton's cafeteria. Clifton's! Here? Clifton's, long gone, was more than a cafeteria—it was Hollywood's dream of Tropi-California: fake indoor waterfalls ran beside palm trees, ferns, and neon orchids. Beneath the restaurant was an underground grotto with a life-sized statue of Jesus praying in a blue-lit garden of Gethsemane. Clifton's was everything one could hope for.

But something is amiss here—my aunt's photo is different from the one I've seen. My father should be closest to the camera, smiling with half-closed eyes, shy and celebratory, boozy and just married. Uncle Harry should be settled into his collar, eyes squeezed shut in reptilian contentment. They should all be there on one side of the table—the American side of my family, the ones I'm told don't like us. Mother sits with them in her satin gown, a tan face in a white row. Mamá, my Mexican grandmother, sits primly in her usual dark dress and pillbox hat. She sits stiffly, a wax effigy, while Ricardo is seen winding an arm around her. Nora leans forward, trying to get in the shot.

But this photo shows a different reception, with attitudes I've never seen: Uncle Harry's eyes are open and glaring into the camera. The candid moment is formalized, with all mouths saying, "Cheese!" All but two. My mother, her head turned away, meets the eyes of Ricardo, who smiles back as though sharing a secret. Dad looks unsuspectingly into the camera, his wedded hand aloft.

Blinking back tears, I push past my aunt and out of the chapel closet. My mother and I came here to get closer together and answer old questions—not raise new ones. I prefer my mother's photo, back in the States.

I almost run into my mother as I rush out of the bedroom.

"What's wrong?" she asks.

I shake my head and wave off her question, but she grips my arm.

"We're leaving right now," she says fiercely. "I called a cab." She says this because she thinks Nora has been rude to me, and she's been waiting for the rudeness all morning. She spies Nora approaching over my shoulder, and they exchange flinty looks.

"I've called a cab," my mother says.

Nora looks mildly surprised but does not protest. She reaches out and clasps my shoulder. "Your mother," she says, shaking her head. "She doesn't want me to be alone with you."

I am wise enough now to know that a nod in this territory too easily becomes an allegiance. I say nothing.

* * *

My mother and I are sitting in the garden room of the Hotel Milano, which is decorated in a kind of Egipto-Azteca style. Stately palms in fat clay pots stretch the length of the room toward a pattering fountain. Tables are tucked in between the trees, obscured from view. The sound of the fountain echoes off the concrete floor and bounces from the frosted skylight. It's slightly chilly.

"This hotel looks the same as in 1940," my mother is saying. "I used to work at the reception desk when I was a teenager."

She has that kind of smile on her face, remembering a past with no connection to its future.

"My hometown," she sighs, "my hometown."

Coming from my mother's mouth, English words like "teenager" and "hometown" have a strange effect on me. "Teenager," carefully enunciated, conjures up beach-blanket-bingo and Annette Funicello movies. Even after many years, Mother said certain words with the kind of delight a social smoker might exhibit blowing a smoke ring at a party. "Teenager" was one of these words. "Hometown" I had never heard her use. Hometown, hometown. The word itself is homey and reminds me of the Midwest and Main Street—far from the garden room of the Hotel Milano. Yet I know her nostalgia and my understanding are rooted in separate places and can do little else but emerge in English.

"I was so shy," she says. "I could barely open my mouth."

"But why didn't you?" I persist.

"They downed me," she says. "What could I do?"

But why did you let them, I silently accuse. Why did you take it, why didn't you let me speak Spanish, why didn't you say yes yes yes I'm Mexican I'm Mexican I'm Mexican! But I can remember the "downing" she's talking about, and now I know how it feels not to speak the language. No matter if she had lived two-thirds of her life in the United States; to Americans she would always be a foreigner.

"Indian!" I remember my dad shouting the word at her during his worst drunk. She sat there, passive, unhearing.

"Look at you there, Indian! Why don't you say something?"

She didn't seem to hear, but I did. What does that make me? I knew my father loved us, but there was something he wanted to wrest from her, face tightly held between his two hands. Now I would do the same, a silent accomplice.

"Did you ever love him?"

"Who?"

"Dad. Who else?"

"I loved him until the day he died," she answers without hesitation. "Or if I didn't," she adds, "I was woman enough to take it."

Somewhere in the back of my head I want to rationalize the mistakes, call them out and loosen the shroud that binds them. Then I'll understand, I say; and when I understand, I'll forgive; and when I forgive, I'll love—without reservation, without question. But in the end my conditional love burdens and frustrates me, and I'm disgusted with my squint-eyed scrutiny.

* * *

There won't be time to go to the Museum of Anthropology. No leisurely stroll past antique fragments, marked and numbered. Votive statue here; flaring vase there. Someone designs a program and develops a chronology—even missing things are allotted a placeholder; reconstructions happen from the lip of a pot, a rudiment of color. I'll put it all aside for another day. Today it is warm and my blouse sticks to a place between my shoulders. Today we leave for Cuernavaca.

* * *

There are tourists in Cuernavaca, American, Japanese,
I see them.
The artists flock here too, more common than fleas,
I know them.
Go to the Palace of Cortés, hear the brass band wheeze,
You'll like them.

See the rich look out from high-walled ease,
I'm not a Socialist; I'd like to be there too.
La Canción del Rey Burgués

I once read a book by an Englishwoman about Cuernavaca just before the Revolution. She talked about the cool, vine-covered patios and the plums as big as your fist. From the looks of the traffic jam in the main plaza, I'd say Cuernavaca has changed quite a bit. But not Hotel Paradiso. The same circle of rooms looking out onto a profusion of greenery, the same spacious dining room, low-lying bungalows, and red-tiled roofs. Mother says only the swimming pool is new. I'm glad we're here and not at a modern, high-tech hotel; I'm glad it's aging and familiar. Still, the knowledge that Nora, Ricardo, Isabel, and my mother were once looking at these same buildings stirs in me an edgy curiosity. Which rooms did they have, and how many rooms at that? What happened outside the ballroom to make Nora and Pilar quarrel? "Your aunt is a jealous woman," Mother is saying. "She probably never gave Ricardo the birthday card you sent him last year." Jealous? Of me? Why?

"That's just the way she is," Mother finishes abruptly.

We cup our eyes and try to look through the dusty window into the old ballroom. All we can see are sheet-covered chairs and tables, a rolled-up rug and a box of discarded pipes and tools. I rub the glass and look hard to see the polished lamps and inlaid chevrons of the '40s, but the dirt seems to be on the inside too.

We turn aside, and from out of the dusk, down the long, vine-covered walkway, an Indian woman in white approaches us. The feather duster she carries is the color of blood oranges. She gets closer, soundlessly. She has a beautiful face, with smoothly carved features.

"Cerrado," she says softly. "This section's been closed a long time."

* * *

It's already dark when our bus pulls into Chilpancingo, on the way to Acapulco. Here and there family lights shine from neatly kept tract homes, and roll-down slats cover the merchants' shops.

Swept, washed, and dreaming, one last stop before the mountains, Chilpancingo is locked in sleep, a town with no past. I look at my mother, and she too is asleep. I have no urge to shake her awake and announce our arrival, no need to ask whether the streets were paved back then, whether or not the hospital had been built yet. When the bus lurches into the station, my mother awakes and smiles sleepily. She gives no reaction when I tell her where we are; she merely nods her head as though to indicate everything is just as it should be. She looks tiny to me, and frail. I want to protect her from the memory of this town.

"We have a ten-minute stop," I say. "Can I get you something?"

She nods noncommittally and I descend from the bus, finding my way past the pinball machines to the snack bar. Hot cocoa would be nice, and perhaps a soft sandwich as well. I tuck a magazine under my arm and pick up a box of what I hope are mints. I know she likes mints.

We eat in the bus, leafing through *Foto Luz* and laughing at the movie stars as we sip our cocoa. I think of my father and am sad it's taken so long to get here, past the distrust, to something simple.

Simple?

"I remember cutting out reviews from newspapers for Ricardo's scrapbook," she says. "All that ink made my hands black."

So she will continue to tell me little bits and pieces, but hang back from the big questions. It's alright. All the important questions have been answered. I've spent many hours with my head on her lap while she stroked my hair, and I know that when the bus pulls out she will lay her head on my shoulder and I will be happy to hold her.

The bus driver announces our departure by dimming the interior lights and folding the door shut. He looks over his shoulder to make sure his four or five passengers are present, winking at us. My mother smiles and says something in Spanish, but she looks a little scared. She moves close to me and makes the sign of the cross on my forehead, chest, and shoulders. Although she must remember the many years I pushed her hand away, she does not hesitate at all.

"In the name of the Father, and of the Son, and of the Holy Ghost, amen."

She says this in a soft, sing-song voice, like how she used to teach me when I was little.

On the "amen" she raises her curled fingers to my lips for me to kiss, which I do. I catch the warm hand and press it to my face. I understand so very little about the things that I think are important, and yet what explanation is needed here?

"God bless you, mi hijita," she says. "And may our Lord be with us."

The bus revs into action, and Mother and I lean together, moving toward the hills.

Agustín, "El Bueno"

Gustavo Chavando

—¡Hijo! ¡Hijo, de mi alma, me la han matado!

Con la angustia y la agitación reflejadas en su rostro matriarcal, mi abuela entró violentamente en mi recámara. Yo estaba en ese momento plácidamente recostado en la cama disfrutando a Sónnica, la cortesana, pero fue tan intempestiva la aparición de mi abuela, que la pobre Sónnica resbaló de mis manos y fue a dar contra el piso polvoso en medio de gran estrépito.

—¿De qué hablas, abuela? ¿A quién mataron? —le pregunté incorporándome asustado.

—¿A quién había de ser? ¡A m'hija Toña, a tu tía!

"¡Caramba! Esto es grave," pensé al momento que giraba sobre las caderas y me sentaba en la orilla de la cama buscando los calcetines.

—Dime, abuela, ¿Quién la mató? —le pregunté amoscado porque temía, sabía, que me iba a soltar todo un rollo.

—¿Quién ha de ser el asesino? —preguntó sin esperar respuesta— Su marido, ese canalla sin entrañas que Dios le dio por esposo.

—No culpes al Señor por las flaquezas de uno, abuela. Bien sabes que la Toña se fue con él por caliente y después tú insististe en que te la dejara como estaba o que se casaran. Y como lo primero no era posible . . .

Un ¡Hum! de despecho se le escapó a mi abuela, y haciendo un gesto de fiera indignación dijo:

—Mejor hubiera sido que no se casaran. Ya ves que el poco hombre ni le hizo nada.

—Yo no sé de eso, abuela. Y, dime, ¿Quién te dijo que Toña está muerta? ¿Ya la viste?

—Nadie . . . Bueno, no, no la he visto, pero mi corazón de madre me lo dice.

—No te entiendo, abuela, hablas como en las telecomedias. Explícate.

—¡Ay!, hijo, mi Toña no aparece desde ayer.

—¿No regresó del trabajo?

—No, m'hijo, ni siquiera se presentó a trabajar. Sus amigas de la fábrica vinieron a preguntar si estaba enferma o por qué había faltado.

—¡Ah chinga! ¿Has hablado con Agustín? El es su marido, él debe saber dónde está su mujer.

—Sí, ya le pregunté, pero el mal hombre niega haberla matado. Dice que no la ha visto desde ayer por la mañana cuando se fue a trabajar.

Recobrando el aplomo y respirando libremente, le dije:

—Bueno, abuela, tal vez no le ha pasado nada. Quizás está con alguna de sus amigas.

—No, hijo, algo le hizo ese malvado. Mi pobre hija ha de estar tirada en algún basurero.

—Abuela, ya no leas la nota roja en los periódicos. Te va a hacer daño.

—¡Qué nota roja ni qué nada! Eres como todos los hombres, un animal, unos a otros se protegen, se aprovechan de que una está vieja y sola para abusar, todos son unos . . .

—Ya abuela, apaga tu radio. ¿Qué quieres que haga?

¿Qué había de querer? Quiero que vayas a poner una demanda en contra de Agustín y te traigas a la policía.

—¡La policía! Espera, abuela —dije pasando saliva al escuchar la palabreja—, yo creo que sería mejor investigar un poco antes de traer a la "perjudicial".

—Si tú no quieres ayudarme, vete al cabrón, yo lo haré sola.

Disgustada dio media vuelta y salió dando fuerte portazo. Terminé de ponerme los calcetines, me calcé los zapatos y con cariño levanté a Sónnica que yacía abierta por la mitad. Después de sacudirle el polvo la coloqué en el librero, me disculpé con Blasco Ibáñez y salí a enterarme de los últimos chismes.

Ya afuera, vi que mi abuela se encontraba a media calle rodeada por un montón de viejas fodongas. Parecía reunión de guacamayas por los colores chillones de sus vestidos y blusas y porque todas hablaban a un tiempo. La mayoría de las mujeres vivía en las casas vecinas y eran comadres de mi abuela. Al reconocerme me lanzaron miradas furibundas. Mi abuela patéticamente se restregaba los ojos húmedos con la punta del delantal grasoso y entre sollozo y sollozo contaba sus penas. Oí que las viejas cuchicheaban entre ellas —lo bastante fuerte para que yo oyera:

—Ahí va ese mal hijo. De seguro se va a ver a la novia.

—Claro, le importa más el cachondeo y el relajo que el dolor de la vieja.

—No me soprendería que él mismo estuviera mezclado en la desaparición de la Toñita.

—¿Ud. cree? ¿A poco?

—¡Cómo no! Si todos sabemos que nunca la pudo ver bien aunque era su tía.

—Tiene Ud. razón. Ahora recuerda que Matildita, la que lava ajeno, me dijo el otro día a la salida de misa que . . .

Ya no quise oír más. Me encaminé hacia la casa de Agustín. Agustín se encontraba sentado a la entrada de su casa, en los escalones. Jugueteaba con una varita de pirul, haciendo dibujos imaginarios en el cemento. Lo acompañaban algunos de sus amigos: Beto, "el loco"; Pedro, "el perico"; Rafael, "el conejo", y otros más que yo no conocía. Todos lo interrogaban y él contestaba atarantado:

— . . . les digo que no sé por qué se fue —explicaba—. Es cierto que antier en la noche tuvimos una "bronca", pero no le hice nada . . .

—Dicen por ahí que nunca le haces nada —dijo "el loco" con mala intención. Todos sonreímos. Agustín no se dio por enterado.

—¿Qué sucedió, Agustín? —le pregunté— ¿por qué pelearon?

—Oh, Pancho, por una pendejada.

—Cuéntanos, Agustín.

—Sí, sí, cuéntanos —sus amigos a coro le insistieron. Agustín se despejó la garganta y comenzó:

—El sábado por la tarde al regresar del trabajo, le di la "raya" completita, ya saben ustedes cómo era de fiera para el dinero. Ni diez pinches pesos para mis cigarrillos me perdonó. Bueno, le entregué la lana y le pedí que se fuera con calma, que era poco y tenía que alcanzar para toda la semana. ¿Y saben qué hizo?

—No, no, ¿qué hizo? —todos preguntamos.

—Pues, el lunes fue de compras. Pero no fue a comprar la comida como debía, fue al centro y se compró una pinche peluca rubia, como la de "Farra-Focets" y unos lentes "Polaroid". En eso se le fue todo el dinero. Cuando regresé del trabajo, bien jodido, y pedí de comer, me dijo que no había nada, que no había alcanzado para el mandado. Eso me encabronó tanto que quise agarrarla a fregadazos, pero al intentarlo, ella se me adelantó: me mordió un brazo, me aventó las tazas sucias, me rasguñó la cara y me tiró dos patadas de "can-fú" que, gracias a Dios, y a que me moví rápido, no me pegó donde quería, pero todavía me duelen los muslos . . .

Todos estábamos disfrutando la historia, cuando el "Quiquis" llegó a todo correr. Tragó aire y dijo alarmado:

—Agustín, ponte a salvo; tu suegra ya fue por los agentes.

A la mención de agentes, todos recordamos que teníamos algo urgente que hacer. Nos despedimos casi inmediatamente. Cuando me iba, Agustín me llamó:

—Oye, Pancho, no te vayas, tú eres de la familia. Tú no tienes nada que temer. Recuerda que sólo Judas Te-mió.

Apreciando su buen humor, pero sin muchas ganas, me quedé a ver qué pasaba.

Media hora más tarde llegó una patrulla llena de azules. Mi abuela venía sentada junto al chofer. El coche se detuvo, mi abuela se bajó y señaló a Agustín con su gordo dedo acusador. Agustín palideció y noté que temblaba, como si hubiese cogido un resfriado de repente. Dos gorilas caminaron hacia él. Yo, por si las dudas, me hice a un lado. Uno de los agentes le preguntó con fingida urbanidad:

—Dígame, joven, ¿es usted Agustín A.?

—Sí, mi jefe, yo soy.

—Bueno, cabrón, ¿nos vas a decir qué hiciste con el cadáver de la "obsisa" o quieres una calentadita primero?

—De verdad, mis jefes, les juro por la virgencita que yo no he matado a nadie. Es sólo la imaginación de mi suegra.

—Ah, ¿sí? —intervino mi abuela— si es sólo mi imaginación, dime entonces por qué mi hija no está aquí. Clarito recuerdo que dijiste el lunes que te ibas a deshacer de ella.

—Dije que me iba a separar, no a deshacer, de ella. Pero lo dije porque estaba enojado. Usted sabe que se gastó el dinero de la semana en la peluca . . .

—¿Y qué? ¿A poco no tenía derecho a satisfacerse un capricho? Desde la maldita hora en que se casó contigo no ha estrenado un vestido nuevo, que digo un vestido, ¡ni calzones!

—Ya suegra, cállese, los señores policías no tienen por qué enterarse . . .

—Cómo que no, cabrón, si a eso venimos —terció un policía con cara de orangután rabioso.

—No tenemos tiempo que perder, o confiesas de volada tu crimen y dónde tiraste el cuerpo, o te sacamos la verdad a chingadazos. Escoge —dijo un agente que se acababa de unir al grupo.

—Ya les dije que no hay nada confesar. Ella se fue porque quiso. Yo no la corrí . . . —estaba explicando Agustín, pero no pudo terminar porque el agente con cara de orangután le soltó un derechazo a la malagueña (derechazo que le envidiaría "Manos de piedra" Durán) en la mera panza.

Agustín se dobló como cáscara de plátano vacía, se le saltaron los ojos al mismo tiempo que abría la boca como pescado fuera del agua.

Un azul que se había quedado dentro del auto —sin duda el jefe— gritó:

—Súbanlo, muchachos. Ya cantará su crimen en la municipal. Ahí hacemos hablar a los mudos y testigos oculares a los ciegos.

Todos rieron. Agustín casi llorando juraba que era inocente, pero no le valió de nada porque de las greñas y a empujones lo metieron al auto. El imploraba:

—Suegra, no deje que me lleven, no sea así, Dios la va a castigar . . .— Esto fue lo último que dijo porque un codazo en plena cara le cortó el habla.

—No le falte a la "seño", cabrón —gruñó el simio engabardinado que le había aflojado los dientes.

—¿Y ese? ¿Nos lo llevamos también? —preguntó otro policía señalándome.

—Echalo pa' dentro —ordenó el jefe— nos puede servir de testigo. Ya ven cómo se resistió a la ley el matón este.

Ya venían por mí, cuando mi abuela los detuvo:

—Ese es mi hijo, déjenlo, muchachos.

—Bueno, si Ud. quiere, pero aprovechando el viaje nos lo podríamos llevar. Le aseguro que se lo regresamos suavecito, como una sedita fina . . .

—No, en otra ocasión, hijos, —dijo mi abuela y agregó— a ése que se llevan háganlo confesar dónde está mi Toña.

—Delo por hecho, "seño" —dijeron los agentes, y partieron a toda velocidad, en medio de gran polvareda, quemando llantas y con la sirena encendida.

* * *

La noticia del arresto de Agustín se regó rápidamente por la colonia. Pequeños grupitos en las esquinas comentaban, con lujo de detalles, cómo mi tío político había sido arrastrado desde el interior de su casa hasta la patrulla, y cómo algunos de los presentes se opusieron al abuso arrojando botellas y piedras a los representantes del desorden público. Claro que lo último era una mentira, pero le daba más importancia a los sucesos y amenizaba la tarde aburrida.

En compañía de Juan Jiménez visité a los padres de Agustín. Pensé que ese era mi deber; después de todo él era esposo de mi tía y siempre se había portado derecho conmigo.

Llegamos y nos invitaron a pasar. Al principio las canijas palabras no me querían salir, pero haciendo de tripas corazón les conté lo que había sucedido. Poco a poco la cólera y la indignación les subía en los rostros aindiados; la violencia y los deseos de venganza inyectaban de sangre sus ojillos rasgados. Hubo un momento en que temí por mi vida. Me di cuenta de que podrían vengarse en mí por lo que mi abuela había hecho. Con temor miré hacia la cabecera de la cama donde sabía se encontraba el inseparable machete y, volteando hacia la puerta, calculé el tiempo que me tomaría alcanzar la calle y librarme de la ira de Huichilobos.

Afortunademente no tuve que correr. Don Sebastián, el padre de Agustín, dijo que era urgente encontrar a la Toña para que dejaran libre a su hijo. Doña Leonor, su mamá, cogió la cobija de lana que Agustín le regaló el Día de las Madres y la metió en una bolsa de nailón junto con una ollita con comida. Se despidió de sus otros hijos y se fue a ver al primogénito a la cárcel.

Don Sebastián, Juan y yo regresamos a la colonia. Pronto nos organizamos para la búsqueda: Juan y su grupo se fueron por las colonias del norte; Demetrio y sus hermanos barrieron el lado sur de la ciudad; a mí me tocaron las colonias del oeste. Allí no me fue difícil encontrar ayuda. Fuimos a todos los lugares que frecuentaba la Toña, les preguntamos por ella a todos los conocidos, visitamos puestos de socorro y hospitales; en fin, nos acabamos las suelas en vano, nadie la había visto, nadie sabía nada.

Al regresar, me enteré que los demás no habían tenido mejor suerte.

Esa noche no dormí bien.

Al día siguiente fui temprano a la escuela industrial y regresé a la hora del almuerzo. Ya daba cuenta de los frijolitos con queso, cuando llamaron a mi puerta. Eran Juan y Demetrio que venían a buscarme. Don Sebastián prefirió esperar en la esquina para evitar un disgusto con mi abuela.

Salimos. Al saludar a Don Sebastián le pregunté si había logrado ver a su hijo. Me contestó que no, que lo tenían incomunicado y sometido a interrogatorio. Callamos porque sabíamos lo que eso significaba: lo estaban golpeando para que confesara lo que ellos querían. Rompí el silencio:

–Bueno, hoy vamos más lejos, quien quita y con suerte . . .

–Seguro, nos encontramos aquí mismo a la noche.

Regresamos descorazonados otra vez. Nadie nos daba razón de Toña. Parecía que se la había tragado la tierra.

Al tercer día de la búsqueda comencé a mirar hacia los basureros; creo que los demás también lo hacían aunque nadie lo mencionara.

Mi abuela iba todos los días a la cárcel a preguntar si ya había confesado el asesino (ya lo llamaba así); y siempre regresaba disgustadísima porque Agustín se negaba a aceptar el crimen que le achacaban. Mi abuela insistía tanto en la culpabilidad de su yerno, que los policías tenían opiniones divididas. Algunos, completamente incapaces de raciocinio, hablaban de llevarlo a la penitenciaría del estado y en el camino aplicarle la "Ley fuga". Otros, más inquisidores que sus compañeros, pensaban nuevas técnicas para forzarlo a firmar su declaración. Los pocos policías conscientes, pensaban que mi abuela estaba loca.

El sábado fuimos a visitar al preso. Se cumplían las 72 horas de arresto y el juez municipal iba a escuchar su caso y a declararlo formalmente preso o a dejarlo libre. Nosotros no habíamos averiguado nada; no sabíamos qué habían logrado los agentes.

El juez escuchó tranquilamente la acusación y pidió pruebas. Al no poderse presentar ninguna, lo declaró en libertad condicional mientras proseguían las investigaciones. Mi abuela puso el grito en el cielo, dijo que eso era una injusticia, un atropello, que todos los hombres éramos iguales, unos animales, que unos a otros nos protegíamos, que nos aprovechábamos que era vieja y . . . El juez le ordenó salir y no pararse por allí a menos que trajera alguna prueba sólida en contra de su yerno. Mi abuela se fue echando pestes contra la Justicia y los hombres.

Agustín se veía terrible: flaco, más que flaco, consumido. Se notaba a leguas que no había comido ni dormido nada; tenía los ojos saltones y los cachetes hundidos. No se había rasurado ni bañado y la pestilencia era insoportable. Traía unos trapos que no eran suyos, le quedaban grandes lo mismo que los zapatos. Se rascaba todo el cuerpo con furia, le faltaban dedos y manos para darse abasto.

—¿Qué te pasa, Agustín? —le pregunté.

—Ando hasta la madre de pulgas.

—¿Cómo te sientes, hijo? —preguntó don Sebastián.

—Mal, jefecito, me madrearon.

—¿Los pinches judiciales?

—Esos putos y los presos también. Hasta la ropa y los zapatos me robaron.

—¡Qué ojetes, carnal! —dijo Juan.

—¿Han sabido algo de Toña? —preguntó Agustín.

—No, nada. ¿Y tú?

Agustín se me quedó viendo fijamente. Me di cuenta de la metida de pata y creo que hasta enrojecí. Llamé un taxi y le di la dirección. Antes de llegar a la colonia, de lejos, vimos a mi abuela. Nos estaba aguardando.

—Cuidado con la vieja, no vaya a tener el fierro escondido —dijo don Sebastián.

Cuando se detuvo el taxi, un camión de pasajeros se paró delante del coche. Del camión descendió la Toña. Al principio nos costó trabajo reconocerla porque Toña era chaparra y fea, y la que estaba delante de nosotros era chaparra y prieta, sí, pero con la peluca rubia y los lentes para el sol parecía un "Angel de Charlie" totonaca.

—¡Chale, güey, es la Toña! —le dijo Demetrio a Juan.

—¡En la madre . . . ! ¡La que se va a armar . . . ! —todos pensamos.

Agustín la reconoció inmediatamente. Vi tanto odio y determinación en sus enrojecidos ojos cuando corrió a su encuentro que pensé la iba a matar, a arrojar al paso de algún camión. Pero no; en cuanto llegó junto a ella se detuvo titubeante. Toña sin pestañar siquiera, le señaló la canasta en el piso y le dijo:

—Por esta vez te perdono, Agustín, pero te advierto: si te pones perro otra vez, te dejo para siempre. Ya me conoces, sabes que tengo muy malas pulgas. Ahora levanta la canasta y sígueme.

Agustín cogió la canasta y con verdadera docilidad canina echó a andar detrás de ella.

Mi abuela abrazó a su hija y chillando de contento bendijo a todos los santos del cielo. Limpiándose las lágrimas se dirigió a Agustín:

—Ya ves, mal hombre, tú no mereces a mi Toña. Es una joya, un alma de Dios, después de todo lo que le has hecho, te perdona. Eres un bruto, un aprovechado, como todos los hombres eres un . . .

Bone Games

Wilfredo Q. Castaño

Dedications

The divinity of light
the falling moonlight
the bleeding womb
the lies flowing
the eyes seeing
the opaque moonlight
hundreds of hands reaching
for the darkness under railroad cars
the panic sounds you make to yourself
as you face sudden death
the sun going down in that woman's
vagina, electricity, the mystery of
existence and sunlight
all these things I dedicate to life
to romance I dedicate my eyes
and cactus I eat with the
stingers not hurting my wings
I circle slowly the water beneath
the desert, maroon blood flowing
in that pounding heart
all these things were listed
malfunctioning machine guns short
glimpses of Jews and Nazis in L.A.,
Protestants and Catholics in Ireland
slugging it out for God
fragile art made from the flames
of burning flesh

all these things were on the list of
dedications and more or less
whichever way you look at it,
the lists full of people
guilty of truth and one lie can
condemn you to restless horses
trotting endlessly at a furious
pace across green grass
you on the back holding onto
political statements and visions or
dreams or maybe just colorful
illusions of red sunsets and ladies
and rainbows strewn freely across
the sky a harp, a chrome harp
atop a heavenly hill as you
zoom in closer you see the
flowers around it and on the
harp you see a list of names
of children almost born and
lists and more lists of poems
and unknown photographers and
paintings and flashing lights and
new names everywhere walking
on the grass

Poem From the Basement

In here the feathers are talking
about pop pop
the return of nothing to say
the illicitness of your conspiracy
piracy concrete vastness
the cape, the fishing line,
can the survival be another
plot, where can we insert
the staples to reach in
to connect the issues the
reality escaping from itself
the corruption of even the simple
bird's song the dreamland in
advanced decay we are in the
dreamland of advanced eagles
rotting in the nest
the mirrors do not lie
the eyes may deceive the desire
to preach about the surrealism
in your big toe darling,
but catch innocence touching navels
in the public transportation system
with hands smoking from an illicit
heat eating the age of this arrival
. . . this fire, this despondent nation
eating itself with someone else's spoon
let's look the other way when the
dead fall off the bar stool and children
assassinate themselves with the prince
frog's testicle, let's turn the pages
of the newspaper as nails are driven
through the coffee, the poison
amputates the mind with the exhibition
of the eye in museums, the narrator
points to the glass case and says
here was their failure and this is

how they lived, here are the skulls of
their hydrogen babies the cold fingers
of their demented elections, here is
the evidence of depleted erection
here are their tears preserved
in gasoline, here was their future
burned with the agony of their own seed rotting
here is the evidence of empires
rising only to fall, here are their,
their lies and their whores
here are their artists,
. . . their leaders and the blood
    of the storm
    here is the story of cargo overturned
here is the decay rampant with lust
here is the song of blasphemous
tyranny here is the innocence
betraying itself and capitulating
to its own suicide, here ladies
and gentlemen is the exit to
the museum

Interluded Excerpt on Reality

With all the necessity to scribble
at all dishonest hours of a spent night
here for seconds
we once held each other
here the night crept in to devour
our own uncertainty about the
European blood
  here I left drops of old

maroon Aztec blood
  there in the solitude
of a lost inspiration we conspire
to flaunt our innocence
there in the blessed sunrise
we awoke chilled by hours of night
desert air to roll over
and wish that our combined psychic
energy could move the logs
into the fire while the warmth
of our passion eluded itself and
we dozed off into a dream sleep
with the sun beating down harder
every second until finally we
kicked aside the blankets and
stood before the growth of air
that flowered and flowed down from
vanishing stars
to stand with us as
we greeted the new sun

The Lantern of Her Caves

Kathleen J. Torres

The Slaughtered Lamb Takes the Sealed Book

> Late sun opening the Book,
> blank page like light,
> invisible words unscrawled,
> impossible syntax
> of apocalypse–
> *Allen Ginsberg*

I

Blue eyes, large pink cheeks,
a German woman in maroon overalls,
she smelled slightly in the yellow shirt.
We walked together toward the cathedral square.
Carriages and cars drove by;
leaves of the young trees brushed our faces.
Eyes meeting, the Spanish kiss,
lightly each cheek to cheek;
spoke our blessings and farewell.
Dusk, larger shadows, dimmer colors,
with a suitcase and knapsack I walked the narrow streets
of Sevilla under balconies, looking in tiled doorways.
The train was to leave at eleven.
At the corner, a group of men,
"Mira la guapa que está caminando rápido."
Eyes unaverted,
suitcases held tight,
I passed another woman, young afraid;
bait to a hungry school of fish.

They chanted at her.
Very fast through dark quiet streets,
I changed sidewalks to avoid the solitary men
standing in front of bars.

II

The train compartment is assured to have
the small plastic blue sofa below
two Frenchmen and a character from Segovia.
We speak in Spanish before the silent hours
between each methodical stop,
each empty station.
Lowland tracks, no turns,
sunlight breaches the sleep of tumbleweeds.

III

Early morning, Madrid
train station: quiet; empty; Atocha,
pensive in apprehensions
between each sip of bottled water . . .
        The young Dutch girl walked to the train with
        her Eurail pass and got her head blown off.
        Three bombs were a gift from ETA last week . . .
unboarding passenger, I stepped slowly toward the metro.
Young German, French vagabonds suffocated
the coarse cement floor near the ticket booths.
Peopled subway—
plainly dressed, a middle-aged man touched my bag.
Walking very fast, he glances back at me.
Smiling, he asks me to breakfast . . .
too friendly, a married man; a father.
I refuse.

IV

Carved dusty white marble,
discolored rail and steps;
I took the elevator.
The doorbell rang slowly,
waking the pensión owner.
Distraught and in her pajamas,
she allowed me to drop my bags in the miniature lobby.
I left for the Retiro,
central park with pines and grass.
Fruit, milk and bread,
I bought breakfast at the shops nearby.
The old people enjoy their business near the park.

V

Eating under the trees on a bench
I watch the sprinklers.
The gardner has waved.
A man walks by and stops at a distance as if
contemplating the scenery.
I relax, he is not facing me.
Passing a few moments, he comes and sits on the bench
next to mine,
staring at me without rest.
Calmly drinking milk from a plastic bag, I finish it.
I leave.

VI

Sitting myself on one of the benches in front of the lake,
kayaks row by, duck keep their distance
while birds and people sit on the cement posts and railing,
postcards for friends.
The sun is warm on my body.
A moving brigade of soldiers dominates the pathway,
blocking the view.

Their unabashed eyes regard my anatomy.
Through the voices of numerous compliments, and giggles,
one says that I am making myself "morena."
I smile without control.
They groan, awed.
I become angry, feeling like an exhibit.

VII

At the travel agent for a plane ticket,
packed with students,
I wait in line for half an hour.
At the counter, they are friendly but slow.
They don't have my ticket,
and giving me a piece of message stationery
with a stamp on it,
they assume that I will meet them at the airport tomorrow.
Helpless and dubious I squeeze through the line of students
with a prayer for my departure.
Like a bluejay in a deciduous forest,
unsteady and out of syntax,
one more day was all I could conceive of Madrid.

VIII

Flowered carpets, wooden floors,
single rooms for six hundred pesetas:
"Pensión de Lujo . . ."
the first room was pink and orange,
I decided to try number five, blue and pink.
For a pastime the smiling lady recommended
that I try the zoo.
Later, the young housekeeper
mentioned that the landlady
was quite crazy.
I took the metro to the zoo.
Situated similarly to an asylum.
Back behind the Spanish pines:

The entrance was managed by an automated young woman
who told me the price quite firmly.
Slothful elephants and deer crowded in
small cement sections with barely enough space to move.
I retreated to el centro
after watching a polar bear
trying to keep itself cool with a trickling sprinkler.

IX

Shopping; my pack filled
with French bread, cheese and fruit.
At the stores nearby,
the windows were filled with ceramic, leather, and clothing,
but most was from India and highly priced.

X

The Rastro, an open flea market,
has tents of rainbow colors, paintings and crowds of people
on Sundays.
Weekdays, small shops were selling and bargaining.
I arrived when stores were beginning to close down.
A young man selling approached me while I glanced at his dresses.
I ask the price.
He answers, then holds my hands and asks how much I want to pay.
He is nice.
I walk away.
He follows.
I stop, he asks me not to leave.
I smile, and walk faster.

XI

Nearsighted, lost in thought,
dirty cobblestones,
I advance toward El Corte Inglés,

stumbling through the cool heaven of crowded mice
in the city's dimming sunlight.

XII

The entrance was filled,
moving quick ants carrying items hunched over.
Famished old women at the steps
held out their palms,
and fixed their eyes toward a broken answer.
Someone grabbed my wrist.
I look down at a woman, dazed, crazed;
a doe caught in a forest fire;
clutching the hand of her child.
"¿Tienes algo para mí, señorita . . . guapa?" she demanded,
holding my wrist tightly.
Feeling my rapid pulse,
through a lethal countenance I frown, then
like a panther attacking with its front leg,
jerk my arm out of her grasp.
Buzzing fluorescent, pushed,
I enter El Corte Inglés,
cheap merchandise on sale,
fans made in Taiwan,
albums for eight hundred pesetas . . .
Wrinkled, cracked in discordance, I leave.
My feet trudge back to the pensión.
I stare at the sidewalk,
brown lines, grey dirt.
A tree immersed in fog,
I feel invisible.
Three widows pass me, dressed in black,
arms clasped; silent.
Finally reaching the hostel's blemished marble,
I push the button for the elevator.
Once inside, there is someone staring at me
intensely, darkly,
a hunted wolf.

Awakened, adrenalin released,
it is my own reflection in the elevator mirror.

Street Faced Woman

Shriveled, turned apple-skinned, face down
you move with drops in air,
wet, cold and heavy.
Without a lamp, or plants on a coffee table
to hide yourself
under the blanket, wall to door comfort,
under the ideal, *Better Homes* magazine;
you have no dwelling,
carry your clothes with you,
push the cart of your possessions at will.
All corners, the stairway bench, the market patio,
are your abodes.
We have skimmed cream from your milk,
driven you to black sidewalks sticky with gum,
by our "Chronicles," our "Givenchy's,"
our disposing sinks.
Murals, painted lines,
show the bars of your breaking cells,
our stifling cages,
which after decades, tightening grasps,
chain us until we are blind no longer.
It is then we feel the red towered clock
wind us to dishevelled edges,
finally incinerated.

May '79: Gas Line

Speedometer at zero,
Engine off, radio on Rock and Roll.
There's an orange car in front,
a light blue one behind,
we are moving toward the brightly numbered
gas pump.
Serious faces handle the red nozzle
like the vent of life.
The man next to me has licked his lips three times.

Crazy, Your Heart or Mine?

Among leaves
lies the red apple
which I devour.
Luscious.
Beat, tap,
your chest rises with each
Patter.
The rain drops on the street
needle asphalt, glisten grey.
Water falls to the page.
Wet pine bark is the color of ink
Threads.
Your hair, saved,
cues, anchors
an emotional view like a
Window.
Two figures lean out
and chant to a mockingbird's charm,
Morning.

The Goddess Within Subterranean Women

Luis Morones Careaga

Introduction

Not only are women repressed but also the Goddess from whom all feminine reality emerges. Also the woman within men. Also the Mexican-American Goddess who is starving beneath the sidewalks of our continent along with the indigenous people who are screaming beneath my too Anglicized Mexican chest. These poems are reflections of this mutilation and oppression in our institutions, relationships, and love-hungry souls.

Dedication

I think that the planting of seeds
is always a feminine, suffering thing
and that the earth sings herself
most clearly under the long golden-black hair
of the two tortured women I love.

There is an indigenous woman from Oaxaca
living in the Tijuana city dump.
She has given birth to several children there.

I dedicate these poems to her
and to Micaela who introduced me
to the Goddess of screaming flowers.

1

I try to love women fully but can't.
Perhaps because a certain look in my eyes
reminds them too much
of the witch-burning Inquisitor.

At moments I so desperately want to make love
to the Goddess that shines through my lover's vagina
but when my penis becomes erect
a column of soldiers rides into her legs
carrying the heads of massacred Native-American women.

It is difficult not to lose my dignity as a man
when I enter a hall full of women
who bend breathing into the mouths
of the feminine corpses
my sex has just paved into the city streets.

I am trying to learn how to stand
without apologizing
when my feet are wearing invisible Nazi boots
that kicked my Jewish grandmothers
into sexual submission.

Sometimes I want to pray
that my only mission in life
be to reach an ejaculation
that makes me equal
to the furious vagina
of my wife.

2

I hear women start screaming beneath the coffee table
as soon as the guests ring the bell.

While they are being introduced,
I see young girls falling into drinks
with their throats cut out.

As the potato chips are being passed
a feminine presence rushes through the room
leaving blood in our glasses.

As hands are being shaken
my feet tremble
on the back of a huge snake
that has already swallowed
half a Goddess.

I see fishes coming out of our mouths
with cocktail baited hooks
tearing through our flesh
that hangs over the hors d'oeuvres.

I hear bones rattling
as the hostess combs her hair
with a comb made of her mother's skeleton.

I see earrings becoming worms
as the women discuss their husbands.

I see suits becoming winding-sheets for corpses
as the men undo their belts
to show us
how many of my daughters
they've screwed today.

3

The beauty of the aging woman
keeps the sun's ancient phallus burning.

It excites the lesbian breasts of the stars
whose silver-streaked hair falls in strands
on the backs of midnight embracers.

The moon fills the crevices in her flesh
with serpentine, glittering rivers
that race with erotic delight
toward the source of her feminine consciousness.

The energy that leaves her dissolving bones
becomes songs that seduce the dream-ears of virgins,
solidifying the urge
on which their burgeoning sex
is about to blossom.

Works

Richard Alexander Lou

Fanged Spit

This cabrón
Made a crack in class
About Mexicans
Being expert car thieves,
And I dull of tongue,
Sat.
"Fuck you, you bastard!"
Shot from my brain
To collide
With my clenched teeth.
And still
I sat there
Throbbing and ashamed
Practicing that line
Waiting
For one more word
From anyone
So that line
Could leap out
Blasting that bigot
Ringing clear
Like a declaration
For the whole world
To hear.
So I
Could be redeemed
As a skilled

Vulgar
Combatant
Ready to fend off
The fanged spit
From my soul,
My family,
Such hate.

One Morning With Resolve, Lissa

I woke up today
To hear
The trees
Lose
Their crackling leaves
Blotted out
By jets
Roaring through
Blue flesh.
I woke up today
To watch
Jagged pieces
Of Sun
Catch hold and die out
On gilded ornaments
From my life.
I woke up today
To learn
Sadat was killed.
I looked
And the Sun
Burned my eyes.
I turned
But could not
Shut them
Out.
Today I woke
To understand
That my Father
Is still dead.
Today
He
Is still
Dead
And I
Am awake
Forever.

Untitleable

I thought
To leap off
My porous self
To wing along
Dipping
Grazing
Hot breath close
To my own
Primordial
Beat.
I stopped,
Clutching at
That precipice
Eyeballs
Running down
Its length.
And so
With a chance
To be nothing
I shrieked
Back
At the razor's
Edge
Afraid
To be cut
But
Not bleed.

Poems

Gabriel de Anda

JAZZ

Part One

Slowly at first
through the morning's fragile and soiled gauze
seeps this child's netherlight-drawn memory
of blood and salt.
Leave now
the orchard of sleep
for the arcade of pencil shavings
                loose change
                and grade-school warnings.
Turn on the light bulb,
and
  hop
    to
      it
        dude: there's enough cracked mirror left
        for you to cut down the stubbly infidels
        in the sanctioned ritual of blade and alcohol.

Good morning Jesus
and downtown Madonna of the dawning wrappers.
Buey-nos dee-ahs,
O Daddy who art in Heaven:
      I need caffeine and the Camel's toke.
      Pharaoh's at the office;
      we both just love to smoke.
Dear mother:

a woman is a sometime thing
but this daily grind is all the time.
I'm bound for the pay-chair
and a patty melt with wine.
Through the streets of L.A. yellow funk;
dixieland madness, mime and junk.
Lay me out a few
lines of Coltrane,
slinky and powdery,
and I'll be awake:
        Music-juice
        and sax sweet argentine.
        Dead-moon blown incarnadine.

Be-bop-a-lu-la
she's got rabies;
she can't answer straight,
got a case of the 'maybes'.
She doesn't seem to know that
I can't think in a linear fashion.
But then again,
she's too busy working the moon-shift
to understand that.
One night
trigger-happy and quivering,
I said: "Momma gitch yer mojo,
        Daddy git yo gun . . ."
She switched to reverse, hissing:
        "You ain't stealin' no one's daughter,
        'cause youse nobody's son!"
Ooo honey,
It hurt me,
kind'a stopped me cold,
sure.
But no more, really,
than the fleas
which inhabit the angel-hair
of my old student bed:
        just a sometime thing,

or rather,
one-time thing.

When I grow older
I'll write her a poem,
sing her a song.
I'll know jazz better then,
and really woo her.
But for now,
I'm tapping my right foot.
I'd like to forget.
I'd like to swallow
the daytime moon,
the shallow moon,
and make her mine.

Part Two

Daytime moon,
gelatinous and lazy:
    illuminate
    this time of waiting.
    (Fields of grainy amber
    sway with autumn's cooling breath:
    the day is winding down to a rest
    around the upcoming bend of calm.)
Wait for a sweetness of the heart
    like the taste of rainwater
    on the heels of a chocolate kiss;
waiting for the music of children
waiting for the melogenic ebb and flow
which announces the wonder of a metered life,
enchanting in its cyclical logic,
the reasoning of dying days,
    of fornicating couples,
    of runny noses,
    of searches for wisdom,
    of broken shoelaces,

of baptisms and funerals,
of the enmity bonding brother to brother,
of toothpicks and decaying teeth,
of Yes and No,
of love itself.
When you wait,
you breathe real slow
and you see all those
beautiful and confusing things
which will not
be waited for.

Part Three

This moon:
fine antique faience,
like the skin behind your ear:
hidden and secret,
unkissable as the distant light
of Antares.
(I worship the curved edge
which seduces,
that closed-eye silhouette
of a chimerical melancholy.)
Nighttide's calculus
weaves a name,
a black ink stain
invisible to the hibernating sun,
concealed from the impatient heart.
Every beauty has a season
vested in the delicate considerations
Attendant to undeclared loves.
Allow the flower its blooming;
let the churning tides
flow with the monthly moon;
accept the lotus petal
revolving in the moonlit waters
over the quiet reflection of felon stars.

Pale and waxing,
this unfulfilled desire is taxing.
Best to let it be
and let it find
its own way.

Part Four

Seven nights a week
in an unlimited engagement:
the last neon-slipper is extinguished
(lost with Cinderella-like finesse).
A junk-jazzed firefly closes down
for the night.

The piano player doesn't notice,
really, he doesn't care.
It's a job.
The final paying customer
rims the dry glass,
tips his wig to the threatening dawn
and sets the shoe
on automatic shuffle;
out the door,
it's sleepy-time.

But listen:
he's playing all the songs
he's learned by rote:
    Tote that bale!
    Whip the slave!
    Center the nail,
    and sweep the grave!
Beauty-wretch guest,
patron-ghost: Ingrate!
Saturate the mathematical point
until it swells with a festering passion,

until not only angels,
but men as well,
can dance upon this pinhead
of desire.

All alone now,
the real music begins.
Hit the road, Jack:
and don't come back no more.

I Captured an Angel

Last night
I captured an angel.

I took her in my arms
by force
and swore aloud
that she would not leave
until she had blessed me.
She cried
she spat
she bit and cursed
pulling the hair on my head
and I biting
the halo on hers.

"But the dawn will come,
and I must go!"
Still I would not let her
ascend the ladder by which
she had arrived
at the foot of my bed.

"Not until thou
has blessed me," I
whispered into her ear.

It was when the morning
began to reveal itself
through the window
of my room
that she finally relented.
My hand on the hollow
of her thigh,
she moaned:
"Blessed thou be!
No longer shall
thy name be Discord.
You are free.
Choose among the stars
for your garland."

I then replied:
"I choose thee!"

Last night
I captured an angel.

Acknowledgments

Acknowledgments

Judges

Short Story Coordinator, Seymour Menton

Carmen Parr
Alejandro Morales
Tey Diana Rebolledo

Poetry Coordinator, María Herrera-Sobek

Beth Miller
Francisco Lomelí
Héctor Orjuela

Readers

Magdalena Andrade
Kathy Kelly
Susan Stein
Teresa Chapa
Ramón Ramírez
Noé Chávez
Helen Viramontes
Yvonne Gordon
Ermelda Hermosillo
Jesús Rodríguez
Manuel Gómez

Editor, 1982–83: Julian Palley
Coordinators: Elizabeth Baez
Rita Gutiérrez

The Department of Spanish and Portuguese is grateful to the following for their help and encouragement:

Chancellor Daniel Aldrich
Vice Chancellor William J. Lillyman
Assistant Chancellor Ramón Curiel
Dean Kendall Bailes
Spanish Department Chair, Dayle Seidenspinner-Núñez
Affirmative Action Officer Carla Espinoza
EOP Officer Manuel Gómez
Dean Jaime Rodríguez
Professor Eloy Rodríguez
Eric MacDonald, Librarian

Ex-Directors of the Contest:

Juan Villegas
Richard Barrutia

Department Secretaries:

Celia Bernal
Tina Metivier

Literary Guild Members:

Tony Luna
Sylvia and Howard Lenhoff
Fred Flores
Rudolfo and Pat Anaya
Jeanne and Roy Giordano
Helen Johnson
Maricela Cortez Adams
Richard Barrutia
Billings and Swarez
Copper and Lybrand
Raymond del Río
O.B. Quijano, M.D.
Ronnie Reyes
Raymond Rangel
Silvas and Eaton
Alejandro Morales